ZaatarDiva

cypher

ZaatarDiva

by Suheir Hammad

Versions of the poems in *ZaatarDiva* have appeared in the journals and books below. I thank each editor and publisher for the opportunity to share my work: *Black Renaissance/Renaissance Noire, DRUMVOICES, Revue, Long Shot, Atlanta Review, Bomb, Fierce, Meridians, Mizna, Listen Up!* (Ballantine), *Post Gibran: Anthology of New Arab-American Writing* (Jusoor Press), *The Poetry of Arab Women* (Interlink Books), *Voices for Peace* (Scribner), *Another World is Possible* (Subway & Elevated Press), *Trauma at Home* (Bison Press), *Sing, Whisper, Shout, Pray!; Feminist Visions for a Just World* (Edge Work), *Russell Simmons Presents Def Poetry Jam on Broadway* (Atria), *Short Fuse* (Rattapallax Press), *Some of My Best Friends* (Amistad) & *Shattering the Stereotypes: Muslim Women Speak Out* (Interlink).

cypher
(A division of Rattapallax Press)
532 La Guardia Place, Suite 353
New York, NY 10012 USA
email: info@rattapallax.com / www.cypherbooks.com

Ram Devineni, Publisher / Willie Perdomo, Editorial Director
Katherine DeBlassie, Senior Editor

Copyright © 2005 by Suheir Hammad. All rights reserved. Printed in the United States of America. No part of this book, e-book or CD may be used or reproduced in any manner whatsoever without written permission except in the case of brief quotations embodied in critical articles or reviews or for radio play. For information, please contact publisher.

Cover photo from the British Museum archive; back cover photo: Tarek Aylouch. Additional beats on CD produced by Beatnick & DJ K-Salaam for Shining Star. Guitar music by Omar Hammad. Mastering by Fed Stesney.

ISBN-13: 978-1-9819131-0-0 (paperback)

LIBRARY OF CONGRESS CATALOGING-IN-PUBLICATION DATA
ZaatarDiva / Suheir Hammad, author;
ISBN-13: 978-1-9819131-0-0 (pbk);
1. Poetry 2. Urban Poetry 3. World Poetry 4. Compact Disk
5. Hip-Hop 6. Spoken-Word 7. Urban Studies & Literature
8. Women Studies 9. Arab-American 10. Palestine 11. Arab
I. Hammad, Suheir. II. Title.

First Edition: November 2005 / LCCN: 2005926126

Suheir Hammad's work has appeared in over a dozen anthologies and numerous publications. Her own books are *Born Palestinian, Born Black* and *Drops of This Story*, both published by Harlem River Press. Suheir has won several awards for her writing, including The Audre Lorde Poetry Award, The Morris Center for Healing Award, a Van Lier Fellowship, and a Sister of Fire Award. She is co-writer and original cast member in the Tony-award winning *Russell Simmons Presents Def Poetry Jam on Broadway*. Her play, *Blood Trinity*, was produced at the New York Hip Hop Theatre Festival. She is from Brooklyn by way of Palestine. For more information visit *www.suheirhammad.com*.

Additional Praise for Suheir Hammad:

Reviews for the Tony-award winning *Russell Simmons Presents Def Poetry Jam on Broadway:*

"Or we would have missed the luminous and seductively uncompromising Suheir Hammad, the Palestinian from Brooklyn, deepening the reach of irony with a poem about a 'random routine check' at the airport." — **Newsday**

"Suheir Hammad proves gracefully sensuous." — **NY Post**

"By far the most eloquent, richest poem is by Suheir Hammad, a Palestinian-American from Brooklyn. "First Writing Since," about the terror attacks, includes an incredible range as Ms. Hammad reveals her own reactions in an uncompromising, poignant performance. Her language is sometimes lyrical ..."
— **New York Times**

Praise on Backcover:
Chicago Sun Times review of the Tony-award winning *Russell Simmons Presents Def Poetry Jam on Broadway.*

San Francisco Bay View review of *Def Poetry Jam on Tour.*

Notes:

Zaatar is a spice mixture found throughout the Levant and often eaten with olive oil and bread. Similar to oregano, each mix of zaatar is unique and may contain sesame seeds, sumac, the biblical hyssop, and other secrets.

Sawah is the title of a song sung by the late Egyptian singer, Abdel Halim Hafiz, written by the poet, Mohamed Hamza. A traveler, a journey man, one who is away.

Bint il neel is the phonetic Arabic for *Daughter of the Nile*, dedicated to the late Egyptian singer Om Kolthom.

Additional Praise for *ZaatarDiva*:

"Suheir Hammad is — as the first Palestinian-American poet to emerge, like an emergency, bringing the full *Otherness* to USA panoply. She's fierce. She is political and the poems are political and she is zaatar and the poems, they are surely spicy as well. She's the jazz of Brooks, the hiphop of Tupac, the humor of Hagedorn. This woman leads the way. Except she won't have us follow — she wants us beside here, shoulder to shoulder, a poem of people striding the world." — **Bob Holman,** editor of *Aloud! Voices from the Nuyorican Poets Cafe*

"Suheir Hammad's poems in *ZaatarDiva* sing Arabic romantic, proclaim Palestinian fervent and pronounce Brooklyn gritty the hard truths of heritage, history and love. The humility and generosity of her poems lament our dead, chant our prayers, entice our love, inspire our revolutions and comfort our distressed eyes. Hammad's musics are the gentle strings our souls need to breathe in the air so toxified by tyrannies large and small. I will cling to this book as realization and salvation."
 — **Elmaz Abinader**, author of *Children of the Roojme.*

"Hammad's compelling voice carries an urgent necessity and an angry honesty, and yet it can also speak tenderly with great compassion. It's a voice we all need to enter, a new reflection for this young and troubled twenty-first century." — **David Mura**, author of *Angels for the Burning* and *The Colors of Desire*

In her rich and true second collection of poems, Suheir Hammad asks and answers the question, what is a ZaatarDiva? The truth she offers readers is fierce, clear, and beautiful. These poems continually find their way through the wretched tangle of the world's inequities and contradictions to a place of lucid and elegant testimony. The poet Suheir Hammad has sharp eyes, full voice, and open hands."
 — **Elizabeth Alexander**, author of *Antebellum Dream Book*

"Anyone reading Suheir Hammad's long awaited second collection of poetry, *ZaatarDiva*, will come to the conclusion, as I did, that when we talk about the future of American poetry we must include the name Suheir Hammad." — **Sapphire**, author of *Push*

Acknowledgements:

I offer humble thanks to my publisher Ram Devineni, whose patience and vision inspire. My editor, Willie Perdomo, the first poet I paid money to hear read, a hero, a mentor and a friend for life.

I offer cool water and gratitude to Glenn Thompson, my first, brave, publisher, and Zoë Anglesey, who championed my work.

Jennifer Priestley, whose faith and love has sustained me.
Tarek Aylouch, for the art of life.
Nancy Yap, who manages poetry.
Stan Lathan and Russell Simmons, thank is an empty word.
Katherine DeBlassie & John Rodriguez, for eyes when my own were weary.
My Orisha family, whose prayers have grown me. Honey.

Let me shine now on Bahia, Alice, Andrew, Lisa, Marie, Danny, Kendra, Sabrina, Nadya, Safi, Kevin, Sandra, Lisa, Nazim, Khidir, Walid, Justin, Gina. It has been a decade since my last book, and there are many who are not listed by name, but whose support is felt and appreciated.

Marwan Saleh whose presence in my life is evident in these pages, and in the pages of a book in the sky, entitled *Grace*.

My father, who is my share in the world. My mother, who is beauty. My brothers, Sameeh and Omar, who inspire my faith and deepen my love. My sisters, Sabrine and Suzan, who are my foundation and ascension.

The cast and crew of *Russell Simmons Presents Def Poetry Jam on Broadway*. Everyone who came to see the show. Every editor who published my work. Every book seller who passed it on. Every teacher who has shared my voice. Every activist who has magnified my contribution. Every critic who was fair. Every hater who only made me stronger. Every website that supported me before and after I had my own. Every peace and justice worker who creates living poetry in the face of destruction. Every poet who has moved me. Everyone who reads these words.

Dedication

The divas who open doors.

My mother, Alieh, who raised me on zaatar and love.

My sisters, Suzan and Sabrine, who walk with me.

The divas who will follow.

In Memoriam

Ralph Wiley
Hassan Hourani

Lord knows I'm gonna walk in Jerusalem
talk in Jerusalem
be in Jerusalem
sing in Jerusalem
High up in Jerusalem when I die

　　　　　As sung by Mahalia Jackson

TABLE OF CONTENTS

bag of zaatar	17
lipstick	18
nothin to waste	20
heifers and heroes	21
4:02 p.m.	23
glitter girl	25
sister star	26
daddy's song	28
sawah	30
bint il neel	32
the missing	35
mama sweet baklava	36
reflection	38
land	39
love poem	40
whole hands	42
brothers keep me up	43
precious	45
be kafee	46
valentine	48
cloud kissing	51
over waffles (on the verge)	52
angels get no maps	55
talisman	59
What I Will	60
mike check	62
letter to anthony (critical resistance)	64
the gift of memory	69
palestinian '98	70
rocks off	72
jerusalem sunday	73
the givers	74
of woman torn	75

ramallah walk	77
post zionism (as it relates to me)	79
my father after	81
'nother man dead (the day tupac was killed)	83
no cover up	85
yesterday's poem	87
some of my best friends	89
leaves and leaving (call october home)	90
brooklyn	92
truth and offering	94
first writing since	98
CD Listing	104

bag of zaatar

brown
paper
bags yellow blue
paper bags white
red paper bags

all tied up
curled string
pretty sumac

open up my bag
out will spill

pieces of colored
glass bits of shells
sea beads broken
some orange peel
cassava leaves velvet
slippers for a china
doll scraps of skin
baby teeth sesame
hair lots of hair

open up and seek
secrets closets
whispers whips hyssop
things deciduous
dead things breathing
things amulets mirrors
cracked seven years
bad luck seven times over

sweet oils sandals
honey rocks and earth
champagne chocolates
good chocolates
music music sweet

open up my bag
tell me what you see

lipstick

she think
i am god
can cover up her truth

always moister longer plumper
shade of the season
glossy one day
matte the next

i am mere methoxycinnamatte
not cinnamon sunrise
silica not splendid plum

she lucky if
lanolin included
for the chap

i promise nothing
offer temporary
color not a new
mouth with new words
nor an old lover
making up
missed kisses

do she think
i will kiss her
cover her breath
with cherries in snow

i am cheap no matter
the package i am
tubed into

not a salve
a false savior
sold over counters
a miracle a new life
with a swivel
of my bottom

i bleed like she
and offer nothing
as real as blood

nothin to waste

you don't waste nothin you
know the worth of bread
cupcakes carrots gummi bears whatever
falls gets picked up and
kissed up to god

and it's new and
fresh again good
enough to eat to
place on the table

and what about cherries busted and
sweet meat what about
stretch of leg tear of
muscle what about
almond surprise jelly jam pumpkin virgin puddin

can she pick herself
up back to the table and
know her worth kiss
herself back kiss
herself back and
up to god

heifers and heroes

where the marlboro man   where
he at   come out
lily belly coward
face me like the man
you supposed to be

where all the cowboys baba
promised were godlike
fearsome and upright
do right citizens

everywhere cancer
the sheriff no
where to be found
the frontier fading
ash trays full

pimps playas gangstas tumble-weed
to fill up hero space now
but the boots too big
for ghetto smoke

i'm looking for your law
your order your
tobacco callused staccato
to round up the bad guys
put the fear of god
at least a gun   into folk

baba would point at the screen
that's a real man
in control of his
cattle   king of his castle
i ride the streets wild

looking for a good western beat
down   country time moonshine
where you at cowboy

you supposed to be here
lassoing this heifer
to safety   looking out for
the republic   fighting

hard loving strong
baba   all gruff voice
nicotine weakness said you
was the man   my skin leathered
waiting for you to show
up   show off your skills

been gone too long
pimping all over   silver
gun metal gold loosies handed
to the poor
like jesus like
solomon like baba

come back cowboy
get off them third world
billboards   marlboro
man   you promised my father
you promised me

dead or alive
you'd come back   and heal
these hoof prints   these spur
tracks you left
on my back

4:02 p.m.

poem supposed to be about
one minute and the lives of three women in it
writing it and up the block
a woman killed
by her husband
poem now about one minute
and the lives of four
women in it

haitian mother

she walks through
town carrying her son's
head — banging it against
her thigh calling out
creole *come see, see what*
they've done to my flesh
holds on to him grip tight
through hair wool
his head all that's
left of her

in tunisia

she folds pay into stocking
washes his european semen
off her head
sings berber *the gold*
haired one favored me, rode
and ripped, i now have food to eat
hands her heart to god and
the month's rent to mother

brooklyn lover

stumbles — streets ragged under sneakers
she carries her heart
banged up crying ghetto
look, look what's been done with
my flesh, my trust, humanity,
somebody tell me
something

glitter girl

paved in diamonds
carved in gold
pussy glitter
the good stuff real thing

know how a mirror breaks
seven years bad luck
breaks into shards sharp edge
glitter like blood
if you touch it
bleed bad luck

that's what happens to girls
too when they get touched
get broken they break
i broke
into shards
flowers into thorn
sharp edge pretty
blood and all

and now
i glitter
still
i shine

sister star

my sister
star
i chose you
wished on a light turned out
to be you

girl from across a room
you calm
i cross miles
your peach smile warms
my back   grove lined
palms open and guiding
me home

reflection
eternal protection
maternal this bond word
made flesh spirit manifest
muscle strength no match
when i fall
you the catch

fly one
when i blue moon
you splendid sun

i shine to reflect
you so you see yourself
beautiful in my eyes

in another world we are
sitting children at our feet
plaiting hair dishing
rice in bowls of female bones

i fear no death
with you in my life

you grace
you sparkle

you forgive those who hurt you
i'll hold your grudge for you

when we need them no more
we'll take our pains
to the river honey
ourselves hum the vibration
we originate from

we've walked through
traps few escape holding hands tracing
the steps before us paving
a way for those who follow

we habibti are one
in ways no words can
illuminate no photo can illustrate

i am witness
to your age your
life in flame

in this brick world i
warm my soul by
your light by your
brilliant light

daddy's song

you always loved classics   said
new music was shit   just
like comedians couldn't make jokes
without getting nasty no more
singers couldn't sing

in your day there was sinatra presley
(you hated him   wouldn't let us watch his flicks)
and some cat   named cooke

all the time
*sam cooke can sing   sam cooke sang real
songs   simple and good*

i was in high school
the first time i heard your mix
tape of cooke classics and
i fell in love with his voice   smooth   smooth

and i fell in love
with the daddy i thought   all
this time talking about
some sinatra presley like guy
not this sweet   sweet music

i was in college when we rented
malcolm's life on video and
the one good thing spike lee ever
did was play that song   your
song as malcolm   i mean denzel
was getting ready to die

you cried   in your easy   boy reclining
your head to better listen   that was you
daddy   born by a river
in a little tent   and i swear
you been running
running ever since

that's my song too daddy
and one day i'm gonna sing it
for you in a poem

sawah

I
if you by chance
come across my beloved
remind him of me
of these eyes and these hands

he will remember me as
a poet and as
a pair of eyes a set
of hands

II
this is what poets do
fall in love over and out

they break hearts poets
do and then wail when
their own are bruised

words carry no weight
meaning is in silence
in the space
between history and hope

they divine watermelon
seeds touch everything
counter philosophies count
on deities poets
live cusping fear

for years they travel
exile a constant
static state
where they live
life is unreal until a kiss

this is the present
they offer

III
when you find my beloved
the dark haired
smiling eyed one
remind him of me of
my laugh and my dance

do not tell him i
have cried nightly for
him waited for him

these words carry no weight

simply remind him
we are poets each
of us travelers between
history and hope

bint il neel

I
no surprise it was your father
started it   taught you allah's
word and said sing daughter
sing

a bird you sang
from your belly to soar over
all of egypt

in the delta's villages
muwlads weddings
ramadan breakfasts   you flew your voice
no surprise

it was god started it
put a burning
in your mouth and said
open up and sing

you were young and a novelty
voice so big   baba dressed you
a boy and you traveled
to the ears

of rich men learned men
men of leisure with shillings and servants
entrances for you to shadow

II
i did not like you
how could i   my mother
would turn off the radio
playing assimilation and press
tape play   always you

first the applause
then the men yelling   always the men
ya aaallaaaahh! praising
your voice   a gift
from paradise

the music always
a long intro
then your voice flying
through the roach speakers of a cheap
plastic radio into brooklyn with
a wailing
a whale of a voice
with words
i
did
not
understand

this was all   your voice
my mother had to remind her
of herself and i
hated you   you
made mommy cry

III
you loved
poetry and god's word

stressed sang juiced a line
until it rang perfect

listen

ya naceeni
oh you who have forgotten
it has never crossed your mind to ask after me

oh you who
have forgotten me
oh
you who have forgotten me
oh you
who have forgotten me
oh
you
who
have
forgotten
me

IV
and now i have made
mama cry   i who
love poetry and
god's good word

i who stress a line
until it sounds
like a note

wa inti ala bali
you are on my mind

i have not forgotten
and though it was men and
their gods started it
you sang for women
for my mother and her daughters

your voice a bird
under her wings
tears not shed
made her heavy   flew low
a breeze from the nile

the missing

the way loss seeps
into neck hollows
and curls at temples

sits between front teeth
cavity empty and waiting
for mourning to open

the way morning stays
forever shadowing vision
shaping lives with memory

a drawer won't close
elusive sleep
smile illusive
the only real is grief

forever counting
the day's minutes
without knowing
so that one day
you find your self

missing that love
like sugar
aches

mama sweet baklava

everyone got a favorite
sweet   every woman
got a recipe

she is baklava
backbone strong foundation
layers thousand layers
upon each other like
refugees fleeing or cold
children warming against each other
holding each other against
stiff hungry winds

thousand and one flaky layers like
her nights and her center
pistachio walnut crushed
years of rough pounded heart
hear her crunch
in the mouths of men

more layers infinite
upon each other pressed
into steel children marriage
nation woman

toothsome and full too much
of her aches stomachs but
at weddings and circumcisions
baklava is tissued and stuffed
into pockets   purses
for coffee later

this woman called arab
alien to her jaw breaker children
of now and laters and bad chocolate

bars too sweet   sticky
blood   the honey   the glaze
final touch before serving
cutting precise   like arched
eyebrows and enough
for everyone

her recipe old and passed
down through word
of hand creating and sustaining
substantial   delicious

one and a thousand chiffon
veils of exile
dispossession   and miles
between her and home

the home where she is
sweet and favorite
her recipe known
and appreciated

the walnut almond home
of her   where she sits
back with strong black
coffee and finally
tastes herself rose
water   sweet
slow   delicious

reflection

nothing   he'd see
nothing in the mirror
of the river
no reflection peering
sweet water flowing

oh   he'd see fish
the moon light sun
light   his mother
beside him warning
don't fall in
but not his own

eyes nose his pretty
mouth ears

for years   nothing

water always ran
one thing he learned
and did   run
trying to catch
sight of himself

he expected
to look into god's mirror
and see man's view

eyes nose ears pretty mouth

all the while god's
daughter   river
was saying *look son*
without falling in see
yourself in the fish
iridescent stop running
your spirit in the sun
look   see your soul
the luminescence
your self
the moon

ZAATARDIVA

land

his approach
to love he said
was that of a farmer

most love like
hunters and like
hunters most kill
what they desire

he tills
soil through toes
nose in the wet
earth he waits
prays to the gods
and slowly harvests
thankful

love poem

it is late raining tonight
the only safe space i know
is the air still warm right after
a kiss the place where lips almost meet
breath lives electric

need is past now i hunger
not in heat but searching
for more than a pyre to sun me and my body
is straining against sleep
close

i want to be open and hide
the children of palestine within me
head first i would bear down
bring them into me
an act of desperate love

the israeli army shoots children in the head

i would shelter them where
it is warm where limbs meet
where life is where babies
come from horizon dawning

pray these children
grow up fall in love
make love everywhere always
be human be alive

it is said sex is
in the head where god is
where too ancestry where
vision and memory
and the ability to hear angels

place palestine's
children in this sacred
air between kisses breathe them in
love them safe until
the israeli army stops
shooting children in the head

whole hands

his hands above
have sheltered and
shaded reflected the
sun encompassed
the moon whole

his hands around
me been bread fed
me kept me
alive simple
warm whole

his hands inside
me playing piano
with broken chords he
tuned up turned
me out whole

and his hands cupped
have caught me as
i fell drop by glisten
fingers coaxing my
arrival whole

brothers keep me up

is your skin still soft
here feel mine   a shine of survival

feel   you left me
wet   love dried on thighs
still aching   you were
sore after the last
time are you still

you broke heart and out
i still light
candles for your safe journey
to the corner   pray your
flesh won't be too brown today
your beauty too offensive

shot for being a spic around a shook cop
lynched for being nigger loud to klan ears
deported cause your name is mohammad and somewhere a bomb went off
drugged up and drunked cause you native to the land and claim birthright

i fear for your life   though no longer in it
wrap a rainbow serpent round you to keep
harm at arm's length
i charm gods to keep you
safe until revolution is over

no longer lay beside   me and still keep me
up at night
is your skin still sot

no longer your fingers   long   strokes   your tongue
insistent welcome

the statistics   political promises
you won't live to see thirty

how many incidents since
we last kissed

don't believe in this
world   so i fight
so you'll live   to love free
who you want   i know that's not me
so i don't call
don't write   take your space
your love back   baby   be safe in it

got you
i got your back even
as i watch my own
from the hurt you left behind

are you soft still

those who would kill
you   send my way
i'll tell them they wrong
you ain't no boy   you man
enough to get up
every morning   despite a reality
created against you   man enough
to break heart fully
and without looking back

i believe in love and
got my own back

writing this and you've
moved on and away

let them talk
about getting over you   over revolution

i believe in love   struggle
by day and sometimes lay
awake at night

do you ever   wonder
if my skin is   still   soft

precious

you would not notice
because you are gone now
but when you are here
i wear no makeup no earrings
when you are near i
don't do my hair up keep
no account of accessories

because i want all my skin
exposed in case
you might be so moved as
to plant a kiss on an earlobe or
kiss my eyelashes with your own

you would not notice
and i have only now realized
because you are gone
and i have nothing
precious as you
to adorn me

be kafee

I
you have given love
in chips   said
place these please in
your pocket   hard
currency against winds
set to blow you down

libra man of sun skin
eyes cosmos   body trunk of root
thank is an empty word
in my mouth thinking

of you
who saw me poor
in resources of self worth
and minted for me kisses
priced me beautiful
said *withdraw this memory*
when the world asks
too much of you

II
there is space
in you no one has touched   parts
you closed off   sealed
with attitude nonchalance a
smile to avert attention

and because you are fun
to look at   fine to touch
women   we who sweep
every corner   often forget
to reach   to search
for your pain

III
my arabic weak
but when   as kids
we'd had enough rice we'd
say *alhumdilallah   be kafee*

place these words please
in a bowl steaming   and sticking
to your ribs   past
into your hurt

rice more precious than green

eat this poem
when you hungry
know you enough
sustaining   soul affirming
your beauty priceless

and i carry you not
in my pocket   i carry
you in my heart

valentine

some kinda funny to put valentine's
in the middle of winter
winter nights come too easy
dark stays too long

in america
everybody hurtin in themselves
and searchin for comfort   for beauty

for one day
you get dressed   look good
splurge   pamper   for one day
you feel loved

and america is your lover
you are safe and warm   your dollars
buy toys   cinnamon candy   burn your mouth

pretend roses   a dozen stems
twenty four hours
can make up for all
you've given out   given up

corner flowers   like poems
especially love poems
ain't birthed natural no more

this year i find myself tryin
to stuff my hurt into a heart
shaped box rocks freezin fingers
gold excavated from my grandmother's mouth

seafood dinners   lizard lingerie   liquor lighters   lonely and open

been snowin grey inside
for so long nothin
has warmed my bones
i look for love american style

vietnam nightmares haunt
veterans and desert storm
rains in the eyes of babies born slow

today the gods
of brooklyn accept
only blood and i
have no more to give

for one day some champagne   chocolate
the perfect   lipstick
somethin to erase me

to fall into a kiss like a river
and fish myself out a new
creature   feathers   strong bones
teeth shiny   thick
legs to stand on   firm   root

i look for warmth within
and find coal

valentine's red and white   thunder
brooklyn's *shango* red
and white bleedin

i will start with myself
then you   will feed
myself   kiss my own
elbow   and hold in my gut
knowin america is

the lover   never was   love
on blankets of small pox
and bondage of chains

i will start
with myself   next you
wishin us both happy
in war times in
no warm times

one day of rest one
day of love one day
of holdin someone
real   some healin

stay warm
create spring
in your heart
start with yourself

cloud kissing

kissing you is grass
under me   feet
in earth   and my futon
no longer single no longer
there even   is this
grass   new and tender under me

i never seen walls
dance until you kissed my eye
lashes and the corners shifted
making room for the sun

this is kissing you
is this still brooklyn

and you here   your lips
shaped like a favorite
cloud   softer than anything
a woman can imagine out
side of her body

in the dead of my heart
winter on paper
stars imploded behind
my eyes   and you rained spring
renamed my sighs butterflies

this is brooklyn in spring
this is a woman in bloom

over waffles (on the verge)

what hurt do i start
with   which scar to expose and explain
its origin   my history

i imagine us on the train   you sitting me saying

*excuses and good morning gentleman   i see you busy and i don't
mean to keep you from being fly, or waste your time   my name is
suheir and i am a veteran of several wars   like most of my people,
i have been left battered by battles i did not elect to participate in
and there is no pension to keep company*

*i am not asking for money sir   some comfort if you got it   and i
won't use it to buy drugs or wine*

*i am tired and this ride so lonely   this outfit, this smile, are a
uniform   armor of cloth and enamel   i was not born a soldier sir
i am a poet and poor at war   can defend myself but would rather
eat watermelon and watch the sky*

*some comfort if you got it   a safe space   and if you too are in
need, this bag here, small and counterfeit, is compact filled with
genuine all i got good stuff and i will share it with*

the daydream over and you
are in front of me   your maple mouth
asking what's wrong   what am i
thinking about   what's
that look for

where do i begin and how
do i say how much room in
our lives for pasts
shaping our daily

and there is something about
your arms   familiar   their
circle round me and the
distance they keep me

how to tell you i see
scars behind your ears
when you smile   and i know
that attitude so well   your
uniform is frayed at the
cuffs   and you too tall
for them pants

how do i   what do i
say when these hands
my own   aided enemies against
me   which finger do i point
with and say look   i know
women like me are called
bitter   bitches   crazy even
rarely survivors

i want you
to know

i am stronger than i appear
enough to walk from
want if it ain't
need   finally
and softer to the touch
than imagined

on the verge of falling
in love   my wounds are
healing into bouquet worthy
tissue flowers   tender buds
gem colored   reflected
in your eyes

how do i end this   there is
nothing special   dramatic about
my life   only that it is
mine and all i have
compact and genuine and
i carry it well   posture correct

look   i am so lonely and
this ride so tired this
smile gets heavy   just some
comfort if you got
it   a safe space

and you
where do you begin

angels get no maps

I
just some wings   heart
and a destiny to find
you mine

i adapted to your
breath while you slept
did you know
i saw heaven in your
smile heard the gospel
in your laugh
you my number
seven   the east

my hip
the hop
finished each other's
thoughts called each other
at the same time
the right time
our conversation rhymed

i'm tryin to write
this as though we ain't
over as though you
comin back
but you never
got a map

busy spreadin
wings let go
my hand

and i have yet to learn how
to say goodbye to those

i love so i write
them poems too late
and everyone who leaves is
everyone who leaves all
over again
this is for you
angel

II
you carry the *kaabah* in your
head the symbol the stone of
the original covenant
between god and man and me
like a good muslim
i circle you seven times
counterclockwise startin
at your right foot and up

you carry *zam zam*
in your belly and like
my mother hagar i
run between
safa and *marwah*
bed stuy and bushwick
lookin for water
sucklin my young
at your well

you came from the island
of sarandils the hills of eden
was your forbidden
fruit weed or malt
do you remember the salt
of the earth your birth

are you the first son
the only son
the last son
the lost son
the sun to my moon
the son who leaves

the son who forgets
you got not map
and this world don't
offer a clue won't
help you get back
to goodbye to good to god
where you come from

and like a good woman
i make *hajj* to your door
a skin for the secrets
of the cosmos lookin
for myself in the black
cloth of your hands
the *medina* of your face

III
and me angel
i'm tryin to write this
in honor of your divinity
but i keep thinkin
'bout how lonely
it is to write 'bout
someone instead of
bein with someone

and i miss your holiness
and all that
but i miss the man
you are and the man
i love

if my love were
enough it would
mend your flight
lighten your load
and remind you
god

seven times i've run
between you and my heart
tryin to help navigate
you love you
enough

alone i write this
and fold my wings over
my belly burnin desert

talisman

it is written
the act of writing
is holy   words are
sacred and your breath
brings out the
god in them

i write these words
quickly   repeat them
softly   to myself
this talisman for you

fold this prayer
around your neck fortify
your back with these
whispers

may you walk ever
loved and in love
know the sun
for warmth the moon
for direction

may these words always
remind you   your breath
is sacred   words
bring out
the god in you

What I Will

I will not
dance to your war
drum. I will
not lend my soul nor
my bones to your war
drum. I will
not dance to your
beating. I know that beat.
It is lifeless. I know
intimately that skin
you are hitting. It
was alive once
hunted stolen
stretched. I will
not dance to your drummed
up war. I will not pop
spin break for you. I
will not hate for you or
even hate you. I will
not kill for you. Especially
I will not die
for you. I will not mourn
the dead with murder nor
suicide. I will not side
with you nor dance to bombs
because everyone else is
dancing. Everyone can be
wrong. Life is a right not
collateral or casual. I
will not forget where
I come from. I

will craft my own drum. Gather my beloved
near and our chanting
will be dancing. Our
humming will be drumming. I
will not be played. I
will not lend my name
nor my rhythm to your
beat. I will dance
and resist and dance and
persist and dance. This heartbeat is louder than
death. Your war drum ain't
louder than this breath.

mike check

one two one two can you
hear me mic check one two

mike checked
my bags at the air
port in a random
routine check

i understand mike i do
you too were altered
that day and most days
most folks operate on
fear often hate this
is   mic check   your
job and i am
always random

i understand it was
folks who looked smelled
maybe prayed like me

can you hear me mike
ruddy blonde buzz
cut with corn flower
eyes and a cross
round your neck

mike check
folks who looked like
you stank so bad the
indians smelled them
mic check   before they landed

they murdered one two
one two as they prayed
spread small pox as alms

mic check yes i
packed my own
bags can you hear
me no they have not
been out of my possession

thanks mike you
have a good day too one
two check mike
check mike

a-yo mike
whose gonna
check you?

letter to anthony (critical resistance)

I
this is not a pre paid
call this is not a poem
this is not a letter written from a woman
on the inside this is a

dear nazim aka nymflow-9 aka
bronx bomber aka anthony aka
42851-054 5812
hey brother i hope
this finds you well and safe

i have carried these words for
months through ports and air
and i still have a hard time
five years later writing
you when i travel

but your letters i take
with me the graffiti you throw
at the end of a dozen
handwritten double sided single
spaced muslim oil scented legal
sheets offer me a home
in polyester hotel rooms

you have never been on an airplane

i think of that often when i try
to help women place words together
into rhymes or lines these women
try to make sense of their lives

what makes me different *i mean*
people actually pay you they say *to*
read some poems and talk? shit i got a lot
say let someone pay me to talk. fuck that
just get me out of here and i'll talk sing dance
shut up if they want

i don't tell them i get
paid just enough for rent
rent means a home even
if you broke it's home

we workshop poems and their stories
are not original or fictional
a woman will tell you
every home she has ever inhabited
has been broken into
starting with her body

i never leave a prison
without my head splitting
down my spine an iron
hand on my lungs

when you call anthony
and that woman's voice says
this is a pre paid call press 5
to accept this call i press 5 count
to 3 take a deep breath and pray
we talk and when the voice
interrupts any intimacy
we've embroidered via phone wires
with *this call is from a federal prison*
we pick up the shards
of our conversation desperate
to finish before the next

II
i have always loved criminals
i tell people who try to shame
me into silence

with words like *television conjugal
college libraries* they say
*can you imagine a library in a nigerian a chinese a
columbian prison do you know what happens
in the world americans are spoiled no idea
how lucky* we are here

even you often write how
your time has offered reflection
meditation deepened your faith
but you 27 and have 10
years to go nowhere how much deeper
you going to get until a system based
on money deems you rehabilitated

i have always loved criminals
and the way you bomb my tag
butterphoenix all across your letters
reminds me our affirmation is
considered vandalism

i have always loved
criminals and not only the thugged
out bravado of rap videos and champagne
popping hustlers but my father
born an arab baby boy
on the forced way out
of his homeland his mother exiled
and pregnant gave birth in a camp

the world pointed and said
palestinians do not exist palestinians

are roaches palestinians are two legged dogs
and israel built jails and weapons and
a history based on the absence of a people
israel made itself holy and chosen
and my existence a crime

so i have always loved criminals
it is a love of self
and i will not cut off any part of
me and place it behind fences and bars
and the fake ass belief
that there is a difference between
the inside and the outside

there is no outside anywhere
anymore just where we are and
what we do while we are here

and there
are people anthony who make a connection
between you puerto rican rhyme slayer beautiful man and
young girls twisted into sex work and these
people nazim they are working to stop prisons
from being economically beneficial to depressed
communities and these people
bronx bomber they imagine a world
where money can't be made off the hurt
of the young the poor the colored the
sexualized the different and these people
nymflow they never heard you
spit lyrics and they won't
see the cut of your brilliance
from these mere words
but these people
42851-054 5812
they believe human
beings can never be reduced

to numbers not in concentration
camps or reservations not in
refugee camps not in schools
and not in jails

these people
brother they resist

i will share these words
with them and i will
in your name and in the names
of all who imagine

stay well
and safe
resist
and love
suheir

the gift of memory

who will mutter
the mighty acts of israel
muster declarations
of shrapnel truth

the dead will they
speak to the silences swallowed
with bulldozed earth

the dead will they
bear skeletal witness
to their own lives remind
us long after headline ink

up rise and search
behind rocks and trees
behind peace and paper
search out god's ear
to whisper the truth
they know

the poets the
doctors the emergency
room politicians
will they report
these acts of gods
ordered by men

the dead will they recite
recall rewind the video tape
if the dead forget
will the living
remember

to remind us we are
reaping what was
sown the dead fruit
of mangled roots

palestinian '98

her question innocent
as a scud missiled direct

after an interview i was
poised   articulate   palestinian

quote
since you brought it up
i'd like to ask why
don't they spend their money
they get so much
on educating rather than arming
their children i've always wondered
end quote

the question kept her up
nights burned a hole in her
soul and since
i was one   in front of her she had
every right to ask

i did nothing
my smile   i did nothing   froze
in   i did nothing   place   i
was aware of my hands
fisting my neck taut
the studio lights on me
i heard myself scream   no
one else did

managed a semblance
of a response something about
education being a priority to them
and did she think their kids walked

around machine guns strapped
ready like settlers did
and i can't speak

for all of them but for myself
i say i am not having this
conversation with you

she said she was a jew and therefore
had every right to ask
the one other
tech in the studio   a black man broke
the ice cold   the silence   asking something
can't remember what   but a knowing
look   appreciation

i did not want to write this
type of poem again   poem
places political before beautiful
but swallowing anger burned
a hole in my soul this poem
has kept me up this poem
will not lend itself easy
to revisionist history
nor to sleep

this poem begging to be
beautiful poised
articulate this poem
palestinian and too late

rocks off

she has hoarded
the stones you've thrown

collected them as jewels
polished with earnest
cut them on her
teeth into museum worth

each with a story
a particular force behind
and each she excused
as it hit forgave in mid air
labeled accident
the aim

but the truth is your target
was specific

under her breast left
her temple right
below her navel

she is marked still
traces of mineral under
lashes on her back
in her belly
she has stored away
the stones cast

and while you were
digging up the earth
for the next
rock to heavy her
eyes look

she has polished cut
she has built a pyramid
of diamonds
a testament
her strength

ZAATARDIVA

jerusalem sunday

jeru
salem
sun
day

three *muezzins* call *idan*
where one's *allah* begins another's
akbar ends inviting the last
to witness mohammad's prophecies

church bells ring the sky
an ocean shade of blue above
christ's tomb and the stones
of this city witness man's weakness

boys run by the torah
strapped to their third eye
ready to rock their prayers

the roofs of this city busy as the streets
the gods of this city crowded and proud

two blind and graying
arab men lead each other through
the old city surer of step than sight

tourists pick olives from the cracks
in the faces of young and graying
women selling mint onions and this
year's oil slicking the ground

this city is wind
breathe it
sharp
this history is blood
swallow it
warm
this sunday is holy
be it
god

HAMMAD

the givers

this is modest beauty
a lowered gaze, muted color
a flutter, shadows
a murmur

i am looking for history
in neon light, billboards
splayed on chests
but this is quiet
beauty

and i need to sit
still, concentrate to hear
the blood below my
feet, the spirits in
the wind, on me

under every stone a myth
behind every branch a prophesy

trees here bear fruit as
sisters bear life
as duty and beauty both
giving and rooted

trees here stand, roots
apart, branches on trunks
necks turned to god
and say, *girl where*
you been what you
bring, drink some tea
we got stories to tell you

# of woman torn

did her skin smell
of *zaatar* her hair
of exploded almonds

between the olive trees
her father lit the match
brothers poured the flammable
the women they watched
the women they tucked
their sex away under
skirts under secrets

in this world
of men and molotovs

family pride laid
between her thighs
honor in her panties

i can only pray light
a candle and hope
you were not raped
he was not rough
a relative a
drunk stranger

i can only hope you were
loved once in his
arms that he touched
you right where you needed
whispered loving
i hope he was sincere

where is he now
where was he when they found
the swelling of your belly
proof of your humanity
when they stuck fists up
inside you to prove you loose

when they beat you blue
ripped the hair out your head
each one by one in the name
of god and land
spit on you and cursed
the evil that is woman

palestine's daughter love
making can be as dangerous
as curfews broken
guerillas hidden

you join now those who won't leave
the earth haunt my sleep
who watch my back
whenever i lay the forced
suicides the dowry deaths

and nora
decapitated by her father
on her forbidden honeymoon he paraded
her head through cairo
to prove his manhood
this is 1997

and i can only hope
you had a special song
a poem memorized a secret
that made you smile

this is a love poem
cause i love
you now woman
who lived in this world
of machetes and sin

i smell your ashes
of *zaatar* and almonds
under my skin
i carry your bones

ramallah walk

i have never seen the bride
gold heavy and made up
step lightly
pumps in mud
after november rain

i have never seen the
boy of six correct the falafel
man saying i am not
a boy mouth in pout

i have never seen
the falafel man who is a man
of other things at other
times smile and say you
are right young brother

i have never
seen myself walk this
clear morning the moon
still visible in the sky

i have
never seen
the sight of a nine year old blinded
the bullet aimed at the brown
worlds in his face

i
have
never

a
morning walk
moon still visible
rain in the air
falafel stepping lightly in oil
the bride who is other
women at other times
mud in a pout
brothers smiling gold at a
woman walking heavy
brown worlds in her face

post zionism (as it relates to me)

my mother has always been
plaiting hair untangling grape
leaves preparing plates
of *mahshi* between prayers
and sharpening machetes

her breath has always been

ancestry deep rooted in sun
in land she raised
children to songs of war
kept the rhythm of faith
always on beat

i have always been
the calamity nightmare come true
problem with no solution
backward dirty other
these are not my words
they have never been

never left been here
standing rush of race in my blood
has quieted to this
stillness and knowing

i have always been
my father always was

refugee nuisance man without
land still is his
survival has always been

and we exist
as reminders

families who argue women
who sin men who
hurt basic people mere spirit
have always been never
perfect and yes sometimes

brothers cut each other to see
blood and sisters
love each other just
cause no one else does ever
has always known different truths
like how the number killed is always
double the official

always been
i had almost forgotten
believed the hype

but i hear the way sabrine
says simply
palestine palestinian
and know

this is nothing new
i have
always we have
always been

my father after

decades of stacking cans
of goya and champagne cola

is wide legged sleeping
exhausted cigarettes crowding
an ashtray his breathing
labored brows stitched into
the *tatreez* of middle age

shrill the phone goes
square nailed hand reaches
for the receiver his eyes still
twilight cotton mouth opens
a gravel throat to answer

his home phone in house
shorts and fresh t-shirt my
father answers with his
employer's name *can i help you?*
catching himself economics
and identity all
stocked up in his body

the call is not for him anyway

holding the receiver out
to omar he lights
another rothmans red
his face flushed

there are people who truly believe
hard work ladders up
to a deserved success

my father believes

so he can't get his head
around what it means what

life means what mortgages mean
what debt and death and interest mean
when does it end the *tak-teek*
tak-teek of clocking in

his displays of corn
flakes and easter baskets are
architectural installations salaries
never funded artistic
vision but fed our
five open bellies each
a finger in the fist
steady on his back

because consumers don't expect
or respect a store manager over forty
my father's hair silver since
i've known him has been
steeped in a box dye

the color buries the bright
of his eyes and sets
his skin wrong

he remembers the employee
schedule and next week's
sale items but forgets when
his dreams became
anchors and failure a deep river

we want to offer our parents
comfort cool water as they sage
transform their dreams into kites
and show them their reflections
in a clear sea

my father turns the volume
up on the tv to noise out
the math in his head and asks
for a glass of ice water to damp
the fire in his chest

'nother man dead (the day tupac was killed)

where the words   to disguise
what i see   make visions palatable   color
these words with a palette more
lady   like

in language not mine
which houses no comfort for me

what this shine eye
girl sees through
bars and barbed wire   prison
prime   real estate
years later   no escape

two years before me attica
was auschwitz is algeria   ripped
naked and stripped humanity forced
to crawl mud like and twenty five years
later war criminals still celebrated

no words to sugar
this up   genocide passes as
eye candy   media hungry for cash
and like cash people are
passed from hand to dirty
hand   open palms   passing sand
through time not mine

      tupac is dead and attica forgotten

in language ugly and time
up where is there space   in hearts
jailed there are no morning   glories

where the rainbow arch
to shine eyes clean of rawanda   bosnia
and iraq   again   fill mouths with angels'
breath   to make forget

memory absorbs like soil
and not one word
erases my earth

no cover up

"...it is no longer South Africa and protest writing. It's myself and myself alone that I have to present. A protest is an excuse, a cover up. I no longer have that and besides, it's the lowest form of writing. Anyone can be justifiably indignant."
                                                            Bessie Head

no cover up this is
what suicide looks like us
what we   what i look
like one eye wide distorted
teeth on side of head
busted ear on top of
nose   brain everywhere   this
is what a gun a trigger
a bullet in a mouth does to a face

this face   uncover us
this is what we look like

i speak only for me
myself and my sisters and we
agree this is our face
what we have done to each
other and even done up   and dipped out
if you look real   real hard
sharp at us you will
find the aesthetics of fear
we find what hurts most beautiful

makeup over decay   memories scar   tissue fresh all raw and pink

and these words abstract
waxing on real life
real people reality this is
suicide what we real
common   everyday people

what we have done
to this face   humanity

people ribbed into boats   millions
die water crossing gassed
to death   drowned to death
slave   burned   married to death
this is us   what we have
done   split children open
bulldozers spread   virgin land   mines

masses of people watched
outside the frame and did nothing
some of us witnessed
some even protested   but most
watched from the road   from the water

we shot ourselves
in the mouth   and here we are

left disfigured uncomfortable   in our own bodies   reality
is this face all fucked up   cause   suicide

i say we cause i can only speak
for myself and i have no more
fingers to point and victim
is a coat no longer warm

what we have
done   people like me   few
of us remembered   some
wrote   even testified   poems
and that's all we have
and here we are again
uncovered   face   all busted   bloodied

look at this face
and what
what have we done

yesterday's poem

i did not write
a poem
i read
some and
took a bath
in lavender and
salted water

i did not write
a poem
my words
were forced
and ugly
i wanted to read
and to make love

i did not make
love or
write i

did think
about it
but i was far from
home and alone

i did not write
home or
call i
soaked my
body to
feel something on my
skin in the dark

i did not write
at all
it was
enough

i was a
live though in some pain
over this world

yesterday i
made a
poem with
my breath
my body
in the dark salt wet
and still alive

some of my best friends

below their crisp skin
but above the pulse
they bear
the numbers
inked onto their ancestors
who chant in their blood
never
again never

they own their own names
they bring rugalach into
my home and share stories
of kids pulling hats in search of horns
we cry and laugh
together in one breath

we look for each other in crowds of flags
loud speakers who silence us our solidarity
angers others who would always
rather war

when we do we
argue with each other the way
we do within our selves

fiercely with the security of knowing
love is larger than our details
these are my people
and we are chosen
family eating darkness
hiccuping light
little by little by light by little by light together

leaves and leaving (call october home)

her daughter releases wood
smoke from her skin rich in scorpio
blood survived the first
flood each new year marks
a circle around her thick bark middle

this the month summer and winter fall
into each other and leave
orange yellow ashes
the vibrancy of death

carry it all coiled in my belly
cut on the cusp of libra tail
tips the scales

tonight it is raining in
the tradition of my parents
who wanted a daughter
not a writer

happy birthday poet
who loves you baby
the way your mama did
under her breast the way your
father did with every breath

leaves and leaving have known
my name intimately

i harvest pumpkins
to offer the river eat
buttered phoenix meat
to celebrate a new year
new cipher for me

i got a new name
secret nobody knows

the cold can't call me
leaving won't know where to find me
october gonna hide me in her bounty

daughter of the falling

brooklyn

sometimes we pose you loud like
a cheap trophy posturing look at me
from the planet of illest mcs and brickest cheese

sometimes quietly we know the streets
is watching our actions recorded
we secret you from those who patrol
our thoughts and study our styles

we leave you in
order to see your beauty from a distance
back home in instants we drop baggage
and settle into our selves

your children travel far and wherever
we are we hear *bk represent*
always the loud-assest

we say if you can make it here
you got nothing to fear

true every hood fashion fly shit
but they come to your streets to make it legit

you got as many stories as streets
as each of us shaped by
your concrete and green

you became the safe jerusalem
for us not chosen
yet did not shelter yusef
hawkins running from hate

if we tell the truth here
we got nothing to fear

you molded heroes
and sent them out on record tours

brooklyn i could write you
forever on every corner
on the backs of handball players
with the exhaust of your buildings
for your exhausted masses i could
write you forever for the absences
and abundances of the childhoods
you gifted us

listen to the way you gallop from my mouth
make folks smile just to hear me talk
cause they trace my cadence
back to you

we always return
like love and heartbreak are one coin two sides
you are your daughters' currency in foreign cities
we always come home
and you always make room
like expandable apartments
filled with immigrants and their labors

you always make room
for our sins and our saviors

you always make room for prodigal daughters
who sometimes talk out loud to our selves
just to hear your stories come out our mouths

truth and offering

I (grief)

comes target
specific comes full
navy blue and black
eye of the storm always
late and fashionable
comes slow
with warning stays
like winter too long
lingers like love
veils my days velvets
me whole

i bow my head
in presence comes
low chariot of rain
comes grief bearing
my name

II (patchwork)

i do not mourn
like others i
enamel nails do
hair keep busy exhaust
my smiles stay late
hoping sleep show soon
before memory
gets my head dress
up my ulcer pop
antacids grate teeth
and flirt twirl giggles

i front
i would like to sleep
for long long time

III (the prayer)

come like the wind the first
harmattan come like a woman
riding a buffalo bare
back come back buffalo
woman mistress of death
watch my back
patron of justice
and cemeteries come
mother of orphans come

die my hair nine
colors of god die
my heart of this hurt
come whirling your
tattered skirt scatter this
madness and leave peace
in your wake

only you *oya*
control ghosts hold my hand mother
as i pray honor
the dead remember the unborn
all that never was
and ever will be

IV (spring eternal)

how do i edit
my life clean it
tight light up
the corners i have
freshened my altars
and reshaped my brows i
have offered coins wine
blood flowers and words

these words like *jinn*
messengers cut from
the stone of my gut
sharp target i have
cut myself on prayers
palms bleeding christ
and open to receive
a new name a
patchwork grief can't tear
demons no longer
in my seams

first writing since

1. there have been no words.
i have not written one word.
no poetry in the ashes south of canal street.
no prose in the refrigerated trucks driving debris and dna.
not one word.

today is a week, and seven is of heavens, gods, science.
evident out my kitchen window is an abstract reality.
sky where once was steel.
smoke where once was flesh.

fire in the city air and i feared for my sister's life in a way never
before. and then, and now, i fear for the rest of us.

first, please god, let it be a mistake, the pilot's heart failed,
the plane's engine died.
then please god, let it be a nightmare, wake me now.
please god, after the second plane, please, don't let it be anyone
who looks like my brothers.

i do not know how bad a life has to break in order to kill.
i have never been so hungry that i willed hunger
i have never been so angry as to want to control a gun over a pen.
not really.
even as a woman, as a palestinian, as a broken human being.
never this broken.

more than ever, i believe there is no difference.
the most privileged nation, most americans do not know
the difference between indians, afghanis, syrians, muslims, sikhs, hindus.
more than ever, there is no difference.

2. thank you korea for kimchi and bibim bob, and corn tea and the
genteel smiles of the wait staff at wonjo — smiles never revealing
the heat of the food or how tired they must be working long midtown
shifts. thank you korea, for the belly craving that brought me into
the city late the night before and diverted my daily train ride into
the world trade center.

there are plenty of thank yous in ny right now.
thank you for my lazy procrastinating late ass.
thank you to the germs that had me call in sick.
thank you, my attitude, you had me fired the week before.
thank you for the train that never came,
the rude nyer who stole my cab going downtown.
thank you for the sense my mama gave me to run.
thank you for my legs, my eyes, my life.

3. the dead are called lost and their families hold up shaky
printouts in front of us through screens smoked up.

we are looking for iris, mother of three. please call with any
information. we are searching for priti, last seen on the 103rd
floor. she was talking to her husband on the phone and the line
went. please help us find george, also known as adel. his family is
waiting for him with his favorite meal. i am looking for my son, who
was delivering coffee. i am looking for my sister girl,
she started her job on monday.

i am looking for peace. i am looking for mercy. i am looking for
evidence of compassion. any evidence of life. i am looking for life.

4. ricardo on the radio said in his accent thick as yuca, "i will
feel so much better when the first bombs drop over there. and my
friends feel the same way."

on my block, a woman was crying in a car parked and stranded in hurt.
i offered comfort, extended a hand she did not see before she said,
"we're gonna burn them so bad, i swear, so bad." my hand went to my
head and my head went to the numbers within it of the dead iraqi
children, the dead in nicaragua. the dead in rwanda who had to vie
with fake sport wrestling for america's attention.

yet when people sent emails saying, this was bound to happen, lets
not forget u.s. transgressions, for half a second i felt resentful.
hold up with that, cause i live here, these are my friends and fam,
and it could have been me in those buildings, and we're not bad

people, do not support america's bullying.
can i just have a half second to feel bad?

if i can find through this exhaust people who were left behind to
mourn and to resist mass murder, i might be alright.

thank you to the woman who saw me brinking my cool and blinking back
tears. she opened her arms before she asked "do you want a hug?" a
big white woman, and her embrace was the kind only people with the
warmth of flesh can offer. i wasn't about to say no to any comfort.
"my brother's in the navy," i said. "and we're arabs".
"wow, you got double trouble." word.

 5. one more person ask me if i knew the hijackers.
one more motherfucker ask me what navy my brother is in.
one more person assume no arabs or muslims were killed.
one more person assume they know me, or that i represent a people.
or that a people represent an evil.
or that evil is as simple as a flag and words on a page.

we did not vilify all white men when mcveigh bombed oklahoma.
america did not give out his family's addresses or where he went to
church. or blame the bible or pat robertson.

and when the networks air footage of palestinians dancing in the
street, there is no apology that hungry children are bribed with
sweets that turn their teeth brown. that correspondents edit images.
that archives are there to facilitate lazy and inaccurate
journalism.

and when we talk about holy books and hooded men and death,
why do we never mention the kkk?

if there are any people on earth who understand
how new york is feeling right now,
they are in the west bank and the gaza strip.

6. today it is ten days. last night bush waged war on a man once
openly funded by the cia. i do not know who is responsible. read too many
books, know too many people to believe what i am told. i don't give a fuck
about bin laden. his vision of the world does not include me or those
i love. and petittions have been going around for years trying to get
the u.s. sponsored taliban out of power. shit is complicated,
and i don't know what to think.

but i know for sure who will pay.

in the world, it will be women, mostly colored and poor. women will
have to bury children, and support themselves through grief.
"either you are with us, or with the terrorists"
meaning keep your people under control and your resistance censored.
meaning we got the loot
and the nukes.

in america, it will be those amongst us who refuse blanket attacks
on the shivering. those of us who work toward social justice, in
support of civil liberties, in opposition to hateful foreign policies.

i have never felt less american and more new yorker — particularly
brooklyn, than these past days. the stars and stripes on all these
cars and apartment windows represent the dead as citizens first
not family members, not lovers.

i feel like my skin is real thin, and that my eyes are only going to
get darker. the future holds little light.

my baby brother is a man now, and on alert, and praying five times a
day that the orders he will take in a few days time are righteous and
will not weigh his soul down from the afterlife he deserves.

both my brothers — my heart stops when i try to pray — not a beat to
disturb my fear. one a rock god, the other a sergeant, and both
palestinian, practicing muslim, gentle men. both born in brooklyn
and their faces are of the archetypal arab man, all eyelashes and
nose and beautiful color and stubborn hair.

what will their lives be like now?

over there is over here.

  7. all day, across the river, the smell of burning rubber and limbs
floats through. the sirens have stopped now.
the advertisers are back on the air.
the rescue workers are traumatized.
the skyline is brought back to human size.
no longer taunting the gods with its height.

i have not cried at all while writing this. i cried when i saw those
buildings collapse on themselves like a broken heart. i have never
owned pain that needs to spread like that. and i cry daily that my
brothers return to our mother safe and whole.

there is no poetry in this. there are causes and effects. there are
symbols and ideologies. mad conspiracy here, and information we will
never know. there is death here, and there are promises of more.

there is life here. anyone reading this is breathing, maybe hurting,
but breathing for sure. and if there is any light to come, it will
shine from the eyes of those who look for peace and justice after the
rubble and rhetoric are cleared and the phoenix has risen.

affirm life.
affirm life.
we got to carry each other now.
you are either with life, or against it.
affirm life.

CD LISTING

1/ **mike check**
2/ **bag of zaatar**
3/ **mama sweet baklava**
4/ **my father after**
5/ **daddy's song** (featuring Mohammad Hammad)
6/ **sawah**
7/ **sister star**
8/ **the givers**
9/ **ramallah walk**
10/ **angels get no maps**
11/ **bint il neel**
12/ **of woman torn**
13/ **jerusalem sunday**
14/ **letter to anthony (critical resistance)**
15/ **love poem**
16/ **over waffles (on the verge)**
17/ **heifers and heroes** (featuring Omar Hammad)
18/ **brooklyn**
19/ **talisman**
20/ **first writing since**
21/ **truth and offering** *

*Additional beats on CD produced by Beatnick & DJ K-Salaam for Shining Star.